"René Vaz opens his powerful new collection, *The Planet of the Dead*, by stating this truth: 'We are required to harm others.' Startlingly, he sets this dictum of damage not in today's war zones, but in art's supposed sanctuary, the MFA classroom—'if a classmate called the police, I would be the first one shot and still // all around me people are dying // one typo // one typo is all it takes and you wear that typo (like your skin).' Vaz maps the 'everyday walk' of art and violence joined together for an artist of color—'Cut, censor, edit, censor, revise, censor, color, censor, write and censor'—in language haunted by longing and burdened with experience. An accounting is made—'With a forced silver knife, I cut away at pieces of me in order to construct a body.' The speaker of these poems has hands raised in self preservation, yes, but also in pointing to a small cold planet: 'I will fill the wilderness of ice, minerals, crystal and bone with the wildflowers that grew in soil that was mine but not mine.' Here is a song of stunning possibility."

— **BARBARA TOMASH**, author of *ARBOREAL* (2014)

The Planet of the Dead

René Vaz

NOMADIC PRESS

OAKLAND
111 FAIRMOUNT AVENUE
OAKLAND, CA 94611

BROOKLYN
475 KENT AVENUE #302
BROOKLYN, NY 11249

WWW.NOMADICPRESS.ORG

MASTHEAD
FOUNDING AND MANAGING EDITOR
J. K. FOWLER

ASSOCIATE EDITOR
MICHAELA MULLIN

DESIGN
J. K. FOWLER

The Planet of the Dead
© 2017 by René Vaz

MISSION STATEMENT
Nomadic Press is a 501 (C)(3) not-for-profit organization that supports the works of emerging and established writers and artists. Through publications (including translations) and performances, Nomadic Press aims to build community among artists and across disciplines.

SUBMISSIONS
Nomadic Press wholeheartedly accepts unsolicited book manuscripts. To submit your work, please visit www.nomadicpress.org/submissions

DISTRIBUTION
Orders by trade bookstores and wholesalers:
Small Press Distribution,
1341 Seventh Street
Berkeley, CA 94701
spd@spdbooks.org
(510) 524-1668 / (800) 869-7553

All rights reserved. No part of this book may be reproduced or transmitted in any form or by any means, electronic or mechanical, without written permission from the publisher. Requests for permission to make copies of any part of the work should be sent to: info@nomadicpress.org.

This book was made possible by a loving community of chosen family and friends, old and new.

For author questions or to book a reading at your bookstore, university/school, or alternative establishment, please send an email to info@nomadicpress.org.

Cover and back artwork by Arthur Johnstone

Published by Nomadic Press, 111 Fairmount Avenue, Oakland, CA 94611

Third printing, 2019

Printed in the United States of America

LIBRARY OF CONGRESS CATALOGING-IN-PUBLICATION DATA

Vaz, René, 1989 –
Title: *The Planet of the Dead*
P. CM.
Summary: Forced to flee a violent, inhospitable America, the poems in The Planet of the Dead hold an unforgiving mirror, forcing us to take an unwavering look at our current police state, proving there is no safety in the classroom or in the streets.

[1. LOVE. 2. QUEER STUDIES. 3. AMERICAN GENERAL.] I. III. TITLE.

2017956262

ISBN: 978-0-9981348-8-8

Edited by Tongo Eisen-Martin and J. K. Fowler

The Planet of the Dead

René Vaz

NOMADIC
PRESS

thank you hate
thank you rage

CONTENTS

PART ONE: BIRTH

- 19 PALABRAS
- 21 WORDS
- 22 AN IMPERFECT TAMALE
- 23 HER SON
- 24 A FAMILY CAR RIDE
- 26 THE WALKING MAN
- 27 A FLOWER VENDOR IN SAN FRANCISCO
- 28 TIMELINE
- 29 THE BLACK MASS

PART TWO: ELECTION YEAR

- 33 2017
- 34 CONVERSATIONS ON THE DAY OF THE ELECTION 1
- 35 CONVERSATION ON THE DAY OF THE ELECTION 2
- 36 CONVERSATIONS ON THE DAY OF THE ELECTIONS 3
- 37 THE DAY AFTER
- 38 THREE WEEKS AFTER
- 39 DEATH OF ART / FREEDOM AFTER THE ELECTION

| 40 | BAD BUTTERFLY |
| 41 | SAFETY PIN |

PART THREE: CLASSROOM BEHAVIOR

45	AND STILL
46	IN A CLASSROOM
47	DID YOU CRY?
48	COURTYARD ROSES
49	IN THE KINGDOM
50	EXILE IN THE KINGDOM

PART FOUR: AMERICAN SUN

55	STATEMENT OF PURPOSE
56	AMERICAN SUN 1
57	AMERICAN SUN 2
58	AMERICAN SUN 3
59	AMERICAN SUN 4
60	AMERICAN SUN 5
61	AN AMERICAN BODY
62	STIGMATA 1

63   THE PLANET OF THE DEAD

64   STIGMATA 2

65   THE DEAD DREAM

66   NAMES

67   THERE

68   ON PLUTO

69   A NEW PLANET

PART ONE
BIRTH

PALABRAS

Este es el consejo que mi madre me da.

Camina, no corras. Si ves los pétalos de una rosa en el aire, corre. Pinta su casa de negro, cuando la quemen, todavía puedes vivir en élla. Si ves a otro con sus manos hasta Plutón, graba por favor. Cuando me deporten, cuida a los perritos, y tu hermano menor. Has heredado la pistola de tu padre, nunca tengas miedo de usarla. Nada está permitido, nada puede ser restaurado. Hay agua profunda en el subsuelo. Metete la camisa y lleva un nudo de Windsor. Dejate crecer la barba para que te parezcas a tu abuelo. No mueras antes que yo. Los perritos necesitan dormir dentro de la casa, hay lobos afuera. No lleves una sudadera con capucha a menos que tenga un emblema de la universidad en ella. Habla en inglés apropiado. Cuando te encuentres con un misógino, golpealo por mí y por tu hermana. Si cortas la garganta de ese hombre, te perdono. No escribas nunca sobre mí. No dejes que te maten.

WORDS

This is the advice my mother gives me.

Walk, don't run. If you see the rose petals in the air, run. Paint your house black. When they burn it down, you can still live in it. If you see another with their hands up to Pluto, please record. When they deport me, take care of the little dogs, watch out for your younger brother. You inherited your father's gun, never be afraid to use it. Nothing is permitted, nothing can be restored. There is water deep underground. Tuck your shirt in and wear a Windsor knot. Grow your beard out so that you look like your grandfather. Don't die before me. The little dogs need to sleep indoors, there are wolves outside. Don't wear a hoodie unless it has a college emblem on it. Speak in proper English. When you encounter a misogynist, punch them for me and your sister. If you slit that man's throat, I forgive you. Don't ever write about me. Don't let them kill you.

AN IMPERFECT TAMALE

Mother,
Kneads the dough
Says,
A silent prayer
Thank you hate,
thank you rage

Mother,
Fills the tamales with;
Queso, rajas, carne, dulce, amor
The hate and rage she carries in her heart

Mother,
Removes the tamales from direct fire,
Leaving them cooked on the inside,
Masa still mushy on the outside

Mother,
Was the original master of death
She had dinner with Santa Muerte at the border
She killed him at his own dinner table

Mother,
Instructs me to place my imperfect tamales
On an open flame,
Watch the leaves char
The masa cook to perfection,
Hard on the outside,
The same way mother instructs me to be

HER SON

This is how she taught you to survive
In the world that was to come
This world

Take the rifle and point it at a deer. Its eyes are on the side of the head so that it sees people at all times. Wait patiently among the brush and the leaves and wait to bless the creature. Shoot the deer you eye in its neck. Watch it dash under branches and thorns into a thicket where it will bleed out.

She teaches you how to skin, carve and peel. This is for survival. The hide covers while the meat sustains while the bones support. This is what she will teach you one hundred times over until you become a man. The man she wants you to be, with pistol, suit and steel.

She says
You inherited your father's gun, never be afraid to use it

A FAMILY CAR RIDE

Mother is driving the speed limit, on her way to take me to school, across town to where I can learn English better.

First sound- then lights
Then a voice- a man's
PULL OVER

He pulls her over, touches her hair, then her keck, asks her;
Where are you going? Where have you been?
Mother is silent.
I imagine mother as a master of death.

SPEAK ENGLISH?
INGLES?

Mother nods and produces California plastic and paper.
I wait for rose petals in the air.

He puts her ID in his pants;
Show me your license, he says.

Mother shakes her head
He touches his gun
Drive, he orders

3 miles, 3 miles is what we get,
3 miles, 3 miles is what we drive.

First sound- then lights
Then a voice—a man's—
PULL OVER

He asks for California plastic
Mother can produce none.

More lights
Then a tow truck

Mother and I are rivers
We are on the side of the freeway, dozens of miles from home
Frozen

We walk to get food and mother prays
Thank you hate,
thank you rage

THE WALKING MAN

My eyes are on the man when they grab him, ask him;
Where are you going, where have you been?
Five to one- five police officers, one man. Me, the zero.
They grab his backpack, pull his hoodie back, touch his hair.
Again; they ask; *Where are you going, where have you been?*
I will not leave until I am certain they will not murder this man.
He protests, he hasn't done anything wrong, he was walking, everyday walking, on the street, from a to b, from a to z, from earth to Mars, from earth to Pluto.
I wait for the rose petals in the air.
The petals mother told me to look out for.
Through glass, metal and wires- I record.
They call me voyeur; *Get that fucking phone out of my face!*
We will arrest you, too
I will not leave until I am certain they will not murder this man.
Guns not drawn, they empty the contents of his backpack onto the ground.
Pick your shit up boy
Hands on their guns, they look towards me, the voyeur; *I told you, stop recording*
The officer says;
He doesn't have anything, give him a ticket for jaywalking, something, anything.

– relief –
– You can breathe –
– I can breathe –
– He can breathe –

A FLOWER VENDOR IN A SAN FRANCISCO NIGHT

Do you see her walking down the street? The woman with flowers and sweet bread in her arms?
There are others like her. Grindin' sunrise to sunset, making an honest dollar, singin' those old songs. They all look like someone's mother.

The others on the streets, the seven of them, they also have flowers and sweet bread in their arms.

The hardest choice of your day will be deciding which flower vendor to buy from.

Who do you acknowledge?
Who do you deny?

TIMELINE

It's because I look at things to try to understand them. There is too much to record. There is too much...

How much goes into a timeline
When all you can do is record
Mother,
Says to record
ALWAYS RECORD
It doesn't matter
What you do
You'll be asked one thousand times

Where are you going?
And
Where have you been?

... There is much ...
... There is too much ...

THE BLACK MASS

The dead people on the ground carry my brother's and sister's faces. I can only hold these hand up for so long. I point them to Pluto, the planet that protects me. The planet of the underworld. The planet of the dead.

Got my hands up and I'm going to tell you a story
I'll tell you of chests, heads and spines filled with bullets
Justice, peace and order were the names etched on them

My hands are up
What will you do?
Throw me, gag me, burn me, hate me, love me, love me, love until silver bullets and copper badges Can love me no longer

Meet with me on Pluto
If there are rose petals in the air
If they're next to bullets and leaves of grass
I'm already there

PART TWO
ELECTION YEAR

2017

Heaven like warm rain
And a mother's breast left unattended

They think we hide knives and harm in our hair and arms
When they are filled with flowers and toy trains and soldiers

How many black and brown boys and girls have died?
Gone missing?

I saw a bird with a torn wing in the park today
And a ranger came to put it down and placed it in

A small cardboard box littered with pink and grey graffiti
That wasn't asked to be painted

I inhale spray paint like medicine
And maybe one day my children too, can breathe

CONVERSATIONS ON THE DAY OF THE ELECTION 1

It's not that dead planets need to be discussed
They've always been spoken of
They've always been felt

I feel them now
In my bones

My skin
It tingles

CONVERSATIONS ON THE DAY OF THE ELECTION 2

I've seen my blood smeared down the alleyways, hanging from the Joshua tree, asking permissions for a simple song, told no, and NO! from the time when I could walk with chubby legs to now when my legs are tired and can no longer run.

It is November. It is cold, hands trembling like the bones and sinew underground. Mother took to the lake when I was twelve, gave me a spade, took it away. Said, *Dig with your hands. Deep holes must be dug to find the water underground.*

Boy me digs till my hands blister, my hands callous, forcing me into a man. I dig until I reach the water underground.

It is black
It is smells like iron
It is our blood

CONVERSATIONS ON THE DAY OF THE ELECTION 3

The night that he is elected I call my mother, the one without a legal status. She asks me, *"Will we be okay? They can't do anything to us, can they?"* I cannot lie to the person who brought me into this world, I reply, *"They can, and they probably will."* I count the seconds of silence between us. Outside I listen to the cars on the freeway next to my apartment. Cars speed by for half a minute before she takes a long sigh, composes herself and says, *"I shouldn't be surprised but I am. I wont say we have a chance because, we've never had one."* I don't correct her; I don't offer anymore words. We are together in our silence for fifty more minutes before we both fall asleep on the phone.

Mother and I are rivers that flow into the sea.

THE DAY AFTER

A TEXT
From BABY SISTER

How are feeling?
Are you okay?

༜

Before class I went in search of water. I bought many gallons to quench a thirst I did not know I had. Filling my belly with the water underground.

I tell them
I need you to be here, for people like me

Yes, yes of course,
they replied.

We sit in a circle and they cry. The professor says words and people cry, one by one. I cannot cry. My belly is full with too much water and I count the minutes until the break, when I can use the bathroom.

THREE WEEKS AFTER

The woman smashes past the bodies in line, pounds a fist and demands justice for a drive-thru drink that has taken too long.
> *Let me speak to your manager!*
> *Yes, yes of course,* the barista who looks like me says.

The woman demands a refund of her money and wounded pride. She will be late to work and doesn't know what she'll tell her boss. The woman gets her money, gets her drink, does not get her pride. She points the barista in the bar, pulling an espresso shot, the one that looks like me.
> *Those people . . . those people,* she mutters.

⁂

The girl that pulls espresso shots looks like me and I look like her. We are rivers. Water strong, fierce, flashing, overflowing. Destructive and protective.

We look forward to winter's rain, even when it is red.

DEATH OF ART /
FREEDOM AFTER THE ELECTION

So,

Do you think you're free to call me spic?
Do you think you're free to call me nigger?

I wore three different shades of black to remind you of what has been permitted,
of what has been restored.

I have taken these hands of mine and cupped them into the shape of seashell.
Water is poured over them.

It slips through my fingers onto concrete made of flesh and bone.
I flay my skin until it is red, white and pink. I carve a target with a knife.

When I dug underground for the hidden water, I found that it was dark.
Dark like my skin, dark like my affliction, dark like my sin.

This skin bruises easily, this skin is cut easily, this skin is poisoned easily.

This is election season; I elect to do what I want.

When bees land I step on them
When butterflies graze my face, I pick their wings.

BAD BUTTERFLY

The butterfly with safety pins in its wings grazes my face.

Tenderly it asks a question it does not answered.
Tenderly it asks for me to acknowledge its purported beauty.

Silver, metal necklaces adorn its neck.
It reminds me that it is not about me.
It reminds me that my song is not my own.

The bad butterfly with safety pins in its wings does not see my armband,
the black with with an embroidered crimson rose.
It sees a flower.
It sees the beauty of the flower.
It wants to sustain itself from the the flower.

The bad butterfly with safety pins in its wings asks me what it can do to save me.

Three times I'll call;
Die for me
Die for me
Die for me, like I would die for you.

The bad butterfly with safety pins in its wings wants to drink from my arm.
The arm with a black armband with a crimson rose on it.

SAFETY PIN

I trace the lines of my skin with a safety pin. The scar will set, the scar will set and I'll trace it over, and over until the blood and the poison inside flows out. I'll collect the blood in a bowl made from the bone I removed from my grand father's grave. I'll walk through the cemetery trees to the seashore. I'll mix the blood with sand to build a sand castle that will be torn down. A storm will rage, the ocean will bellow and I'll build that castle of sand again.

This castle of sand is fragile.
This castle of sand becomes glass.
This castle of sand requires tributes of blood.
This castle of sand is my home.
This castle of sand requires reinforcement.

I hold out a safety pin for you to prick your skin, bleed with me, if even for a little. Sit with me, enjoy this ocean, this sunset, this castle of sand built from my blood.

PART THREE
CLASSROOM BEHAVIOR

AND STILL

All around me, people are dying/ classmates call out against censorship, while my brown and black body continues to be censored / My brown and black body does not get a safe space / it will never get a safe space / if a classmate called the police, I would be the first one shot and still / all around me people are dying / one typo // one typo is all it takes and you wear that typo / like your skin / as stigmata / my professor tells me to read *Citizen* / and classmates will still claim that everything is perfect / everything is safe and still / all around me, people are dying / my censorship is my railroad track poem/ my barrio poem / my favela poem / I am a conspiracy theorist if I say people are dying / I'm called a liar and still / All around me, people are dying / will you censor me like they've censored the others? / and still…

IN A CLASSROOM

There is another boy in the room that looks like you (YES, LIKE YOU)

Doppelganger and othered other
Ghost and specter
Emulation and simulation

And you hate each other.
Dark skin, hair, eyes, and eyelashes as long as yours.

When he smiles
You don't smile back.

When he attacks on paper for five months and you do nothing.
Say nothing.
Are nothing.

His pen marks are red like the rose petals as he mutilates words.
You hate him and he hates you.

Regardless,
And together
You both are rivers.

DID YOU CRY?

Precipice of an M.F.A. classroom

On the night of November 9th, did you cry?
If you cried // know that'd I cried with you

When you look into the mirror // what do you see?
Glass becomes shattered // pieces become sand // sand becomes specks

Spic?

The words sound so similar // is that the word you say // under your breath //
under your hoodie // when you see me in the halls // down the hill //
in the room?
Did you call me that?

SEN-SI-TIVE
Is what you write on my paper
SENSE-LESS-NESS
Is the word I cannot bring myself to write on yours

What are you hiding?
Where are you going?
Where have you been?

How often do you stay up at night looking at the words
you've arranged in sentences?
Are you looking at your hands?
Are your hands // your words //
WORTHY?

Are you a slave to the words on the paper?
Do you // imagine me wearing your words?
What does a photograph of that look like?

COURTYARD ROSES

Because the other will other you
The workshop is inheritably violent
You write
We are required to harm others

You spoke to the boy that looks like you one day, after class, after poetry. You sat on a bench, in a courtyard.
What was it that you wanted?

Closure, perhaps a diagnosis that he, you, or you both were ill in a way. You sat across him and spoke for half an hour.

Glass becomes shattered, pieces become sand, sand becomes specks.
What broken pieces were you looking for after 8 months of abuse?

You shook hands, giving burial to something that was dead the moment it started. You imagine dead roses growing from his hand.

Your skin pigments are similar in hue and it is with that resemblance that you repel each other like atoms of the same charge.

IN THE KINGDOM

I cannot begin to articulate the level of complexity of all this around me. I want to flee into the frozen wilderness that I have envisioned, created. This collection is taking the shape of my heart and exile. There is no nuance, but rather an erasure of my being and art.

I am living in the kingdom of sorrow.

EXILE IN THE KINGDOM

I am homesick inside my own home
    Who are you?

Remember, that I inhabited a house painted black three times over
    What are you doing here?

I am stranger in the land of the living
    You don't belong here!

I'm told to go home
    Get out!

And still

PART FOUR
THE AMERICAN SUN

STATEMENT OF PURPOSE

This american flag is constructed from flayed skin.
I hear the bells of sorrow.
I see the rose petals in the air.

Forcibly, I'm given a knife.
Instructed to cut away at the pieces of me in order to construct a body that will survive the journey; Harshness and reality of cold space.

I become a machine.

I will slit my own throat.
I will flee into the wilderness.
I will die and be reborn on the planet of the dead.

AMERICAN SUN 1

You are born here and not here. Your skin is kissed by the same sun, the same blade, the same gun.
You are leaving. You were born here, and now you are leaving.
You look towards another planet for guidance. The small one, with the heart, a wound, the small one made of ice and death.

The world wants nothing but to burn you
String you up on that fire and light you ablaze

You must flee at once

Over the moons, past the planets, past the oceans, past the asteroids belt you find your way to the wilderness of Pluto.

AMERICAN SUN 2

Once,

As a child, I was led by the hand to the rose gardens. I was lined up with someone that looked like me, and someone that looked like my father. Was this the first time they had lined us up?

It was the first time they were caught, recorded.
I remember mother's words
Always record

As we were flayed, burned, hanged, and loved.

We were buried in deep holes, so deep I could feel the ice underground. In those deep holes our bodies fed, constructed and grew their rosebushes.

Flowers.
That grew
Red, black and blue.

AMERICAN SUN 3

We are required to harm others. Even when we carry the most beautiful of intentions, we cannot avoid our nature. We are required to harm others. It is a right of passage. It is part of being human. We are required to walk in the wasteland, when April comes so cruelly on earth.

AMERICAN SUN 4

In what ways do you
Dismember yourself?
Dear, american sun
To feel
American?

Do you
Offer as sacrament
The tip of your fingertip?
The tip of your pen?

Do you remove an eye?
Do you
Pledge

To the
Red, black and blue?

What do you
Use to fill in the scar on your right shoulder?
The mark that you were born on the periphery
Wound on your shoulder
Heart on Pluto

Where are you going?
And
Where have you been?

AMERICAN SUN 5

Let's imagine that the world is pure, where there is less speculation, less bodies buried at the border and less sons hanging from trees. Imagine there are seats at the table for boys that look like me and upward mobility is indeed tied to accomplishments. Where, the family mausoleum is empty and all rooms, including yours, have windows.

AN AMERICAN BODY

Because, you're not a person in that regard
You are a body

Your body is nothing more than a machine, you were born to serve, to knead, to plow, to pick, to push, to cart, to jump, to crawl, to work, to burn, to die.

They call you trespasser, vandal, instigator, thief, unkind, unwelcomed
Leviathan and behemoth
A burned effigy in the classroom

Your hands were up the moment you were born; the moment you began to share space with space that was not yours
Yours is a refugee heart in your own home

You painted your house many shades of black, caking it over until it started to crumble, piece by piece

Your skin has committed every sin
You are the american sun
Your citizenship is from far away

STIGMATA

Wear your skin like it's wrong
Chosen
Wear it like a
(TYPO)

The laws of language and men are meant to be broken
Write it like a (TYPO)
Dark hair, dark eyes, dark skin
You too, are perfect

Mark of the chosen
Violence on skin
Dear american sun,
Your existence is stigmata

THE PLANET OF THE DEAD

HANDS UP!

My hands are up towards Pluto
The planet that is not a planet
I am a person that is not a person.

My hands towards that small planet
Heart wound on its side
Remember the mark on your right shoulder?

A refugee of death
I am not welcome here and so I
Flee

STIGMATA 2

My skin
Is chosen
My skin
like a tattoo, like stigmata, like sin,
Bruises and cuts easily

Sometimes
when I walk home at night, with my hoodie pulled up and my headphones in my ears
I imagine bullets like leaves of grass and rose petals in the air

Sometimes
I walk down the halls with my hands up
For good measure

Sometimes
I am told to write, and write and write more
Cut, censor, edit, censor, revise, censor, color, censor, write and censor

Sometimes
All the time
There are others
With knives and guns
And words

THE DEAD DREAM

They are the souls that slept inside their black homes when they came to burn them down
On Pluto, the dead dream
I am an accidental medium
They call to earth, and welcome all new souls
On Pluto, the dead are allowed their dreams
The dead dream
Their souls rage and
Burn

NAMES

People on earth call out *SAY THEIR NAMES*
How many names have been added this year? The year before? Next year?

This is the performance of trauma
Pain on the stage, calling out names
Their names have been said, and said and said

There are many
There are *too* many

But you promised to record
Always record

THERE

Far away,
Do you feel welcomed?
No VISA in hand?

Does your life not matter here?
Past the asteroid belt, you are pelted by cosmic metals now
Will there be a wall of ICE
Like on Earth before

Have you found the water underground?
Have you painted your house black?
Will they burn this down too?

ON PLUTO

It's quiet here

I am alone

I dug underground until I found the blood and water

I removed an eye

I fasted for an entire revolution around the sun

I found god

I killed god

I am no better than all the others on earth

It's quiet here

I am alone

A NEW PLANET

There is an inequality in the galaxy
You fled the earth and what did you find on Pluto?
Here you found that water is deep, all houses can be black, trees are hollow, grass grows like ice and still

Oh, dear american sun.

You will be buried on the Planet of the Dead

*Has heredado la pistola de tu padre,
nunca tengas miedo de usarla*

ACKNOWLEDGEMENTS

This book was crafted during a time of strife. I give thanks to those who supported me, my family members, my colleagues, my friends, and Dae.

Thank you hate, thank you rage.

RENÉ VAZ is a Bay Area writer. He curates the reading series Voz Sin Tinta and Nomadic Press Uptown Fridays. He is a lecturer at San Francisco State University for the Latino Studies department and is committed to providing space for people of color / marginalized voices. He holds an M.A. and M.F.A. in English and Creative Writing from San Francisco State University.